Bey… nism

A Christian Vision for Embracing Racial Diversity in Our Schools

Anjali Kanagaratnam
Curate, Bybrook Benefice, Wiltshire

GROVE BOOKS LIMITED
RIDLEY HALL RD CAMBRIDGE CB3 9HU

Contents

AADE

Anglican Association of Directors of Education

Acknowledgments

I am grateful to Andy Wolfe, Emily Norman, Bola-Alysia Ayonrinde and Elizabeth Olulari for all their wisdom and support in the writing of this text. This book is dedicated to my children, husband and parents who have shared my journey and taught me so much about faith, race and identity.

First Impression July 2023

ISSN 2041-0964

ISBN 978 1 78827 327 5

A Turning Point

1

In the end, it was the teacher's comment about 'curry muncher' that got me.

Recounting his day at school, my son was bewildered that his teacher should so light-heartedly mention that his older brother's classmates called him a 'curry muncher.' Why, he wondered, had action not been taken to prevent this from being repeated, and why was his teacher sharing this with him in such a casual manner?

Racial microaggressions and misplaced humour with racist undertones are a reality, to a lesser or greater extent, for any person of colour living in the UK. However, this was not a one-off event. It was another incident to add to the growing pile of racial slurs, insults and other subtle exclusionary behaviours that my children had faced in a school in which the unseen code of normative whiteness operated. The trauma of repeated racial 'othering' affected one of my children so deeply that they refused to go to school and said that they hated the colour of their skin.

Racial microaggressions are a reality for any person of colour living in the UK

My children were very reluctant to report these incidents, worried that if action was taken against the perpetrators, they would then have to deal with the consequences that followed. In a school where the norm is white, it is not difficult to work out who 'snitched' on you for making racist comments.

We did finally act in relation to the 'curry muncher' comment. Some members of staff took swift action and dealt with the incident; one member of senior staff really listened to us and tried to engage with the much larger problem at hand. However, it felt that the school, as a whole, preferred to hide behind comments such as 'We take racism seriously' and 'Racism is not a problem in the school.'

My own experience as a secondary school teacher had shown me that pupils could often look for difference in their peers and use it in a negative way; skin colour just happened to be what was 'different' about my kids. I had not been prepared, though, for the sheer number of these comments, some of which were made by those in authority.

The Power of Normative Whiteness in the Education System

Since moving to the UK as an 11-year-old, I have almost constantly been part of the British educational system: first as a student and then as an RE teacher, a parent and a governor. I have been involved in parent groups, been a parent helper and am now involved in school as a priest. I believe passionately in the value of our educational system to enable each child to fulfil their potential in an environment that allows them to flourish. This was part of my Christian calling as a teacher and, as Wolfe and Swaner argue in *Flourishing Together:*

> Our inherent goal as education professionals will be to build institutions that enable human flourishing...we are all called to flourish...This is true for...our students, for us leaders and teachers and for our schools and communities.[1]

My children's experience showed me that covert racism within the educational system was an obstacle to this. This was echoed in countless books and articles on issues of race, identity and faith, showing that these were not isolated incidents. The statement that 'Education remains a primary area for both the maintenance of entrenched stereotyping and discrimination, on the one hand, and anti-racist activity on the other,'[2] expressed so well the conflicting agendas that I had witnessed myself within the school system.[3] These issues prevent the flourishing of many students and teachers of minority ethnic heritage, ultimately impacting the whole community.

Moving Beyond Tokenism

Normative whiteness has a power in the education system—one that can sometimes hide behind tokenistic endeavours towards racial diversity, whilst failing to address the racial injustice and inequality that still exists in many of our schools. Photos of racially diverse people on school prospectuses and websites are not enough. These are merely a step in the right direction—and sometimes just be a veneer that hides a lived reality where difference is not truly valued.

American civil right activist, DeRay McKesson, hit the nail on the head when he commented that, 'Diversity is about bodies, inclusion is about culture.'[4] Embracing racial diversity is not a tick-box exercise where you have people who look different but who largely assimilate into the dominant Western culture. That is tokenism. True embrace of racial diversity is about having a culture that values and celebrates difference; one that enables all people from minority ethnic backgrounds to be themselves and express their difference; and for the dominant culture to be changed through their presence.

The purpose of this booklet is, therefore, to offer a Christian vision for embracing diversity in our schools that moves beyond tokenism to create such a culture. In this book I will argue that the imperative to embrace racial diversity is part of God's vision for the church and humanity. An analysis of Miroslav Volf's metaphor of 'embrace' will explore what it means to truly embrace the other. I will then consider what this embrace of racial diversity looks like in the school context, reflecting on the Church of England's *Vision for Education* and the legislative framework that underpins the current drive towards racial diversity. I will finally explore some practical ways in which schools can build a culture that truly embraces racial diversity.

First, though, some more of my story…

Assimilating and Becoming the 'Good Immigrant'

When I started secondary school in the UK, the advantages of my westernized, educated, Christian upbringing in Sri Lanka meant that I had some tools to fit into the dominant school culture around me. I was one of a handful of non-whites in my school and soon learnt that assimilation into the dominant culture was the best way to survival and success.

I was happy at school, studying hard and throwing myself into the life of the school, a pattern that continued through university and into teaching. I became what Nikesh Shukla terms the 'good immigrant.'[5] However, on reflection, I realize that this quest for identity and belonging was a chameleon-like existence, where the Tamil side of me was largely hidden to most people with whom I related on a daily basis. For the most part, this was a peaceful coexistence of cultures—a private *versus* public identity. I did what I needed to and did not challenge the *status quo*. When there was conflict, conformist by nature, I toed the line and was careful about rocking the boat.

There were times where aspects of my ethnic identity were celebrated but there were many more occasions where my Tamil identity stood in opposition to the normative Western liberal view. I soon learnt that the latter was accepted as superior—what many writers on this topic term 'white supremacy.'[6] So, whether I was in the classroom, staff room or a governors' meeting, I would often carefully edit what I would say to make it more palatable, if indeed I chose to say anything at all. Staying silent was often the easier option.

This was compounded by what Robin DiAngelo terms 'white fragility,' the fragility that exists when white people speak about race.[7] I learnt that it was generally unwise to speak about race, especially more contentious issues, as it almost always ended badly: at best, your experience was diminished; at worst, you were accused of using the 'race card' or you upset people.

However, the experiences of my children compelled me to speak out. For the first time in my life, I was forced to talk about race. I still hated doing it but, as a mother, I could no longer stand by and watch my children's pain without doing something about it.

The counter-story is a tool used by minority communities to speak of their own lived experiences, in order to challenge widely accepted ideas and help people understand the way things really are. I have offered a snapshot of my own journey with the concept of racial diversity within the school system in the UK, to illustrate the complexity of the narrative surrounding race, identity and belonging. I also offer my story to show that this kind of racial othering still happens and that there can often be a disparity between rhetoric and reality.

Questions for Reflection

- What do you understand by the phrase 'normative whiteness'? To what extent do you recognize it in your school context?
- How can diversity become tokenistic? How can this mask covert or systemic racism in a school context?
- In what ways can a school be covertly racist while championing anti-racism? Would you be able to challenge subtle acts of exclusion in your context?

A Christian Vision for Racial Diversity

2

At the heart of the pursuit to embrace racial diversity lies a competing set of agendas. On the one hand is the desire to preserve our own identity, the human inclination to gravitate toward those who are like us and understand our struggle to deal with difference or otherness. On the other hand is the desire to treat everyone the same, irrespective of race. The Christian vision for embracing racial diversity deepens this desire and articulates a God-given imperative to embrace racial diversity in all communities.

What Does the Bible Say About Racial Diversity?

In many ways it is easy to discern what the Bible says about racial diversity. My years teaching GCSE RE showed that complex religious issues were often simplified and distilled into a few key beliefs, such as this quotation from BBC Bitesize: 'Christians believe that all humans are made in the image of God. Therefore, any action that devalues a person is an insult to God who created and loves that person.'[8] This draws on the foundational truth of the Genesis creation narrative, illustrating that the belief in God as creator (who creates humans in his image) and God as Father (in which all humans are his children) should always be the starting point for any theological conversation on race.

Racial diversity pulses through the biblical story from beginning to end. Christians believe that it is the triune God (God as three in one) who creates a diverse world and humans are made in the image of God, whose very nature is unity in diversity. As Paul explains in Acts 17.26, differences between people groups are part of God's intention: 'From one man [God] made all nations that they should inhabit the whole earth.' Even God's special covenant relationship with Abraham (and therefore with Israel) was a means by which God's grace could flow to all nations (Gen 12.3). This vision of unity in diversity finds its culmination at the end of the story in Revelation, which envisions the end of time, where 'every nation, tribe, people and language' are united in worshipping Jesus, the lamb (Rev 7.9-10).

Applying this big picture in the Bible is a reminder that each student (and member of staff) is a precious human made in the image of God, equal in status and equally loved by God. Moreover, the racial (and other) differences that make up each classroom and school community are part of God's intention in creation and are to be embraced and celebrated.

The teaching on racial diversity is clear: it is the way God intended it. So, what is the problem? Let us go back to that BBC Bitesize quotation: 'Any action that devalues a person is an insult to God…' And there we have it! As history has shown, the issue is not with what the Bible teaches but with the way in which it is interpreted. Any action that devalues another person is sinful. Racism (and any other form of discrimination) is particularly problematic because the devaluing of a person is based on difference and an ideology—whether conscious or unconscious—that one people group is in some way superior.

Rather than devaluing people because of their difference, embracing racial diversity is about valuing that difference. It is about unity in diversity: celebrating our differences and learning from each other.

The Problem of Language

None of the Bible verses talk about race; they talk about nations, tribes and languages but not races. This is because the issue of race as we understand it, and especially the ordering of people according to the colour of their skin, is a relatively modern idea. This racial logic is a product of Enlightenment thinking and was used by philosophers and theologians as a way of justifying their countries' colonial endeavours. A belief in white supremacy was used to justify the oppression of darker skinned people and, worryingly, as theologians such as Jennings and Carter argue, this logic found its roots in Christian theology itself.[9]

Race is therefore a social construct and it can be argued that using the terminology of race in describing various people groups is problematic as it continues to perpetuate an ideology that is problematic.[10] Some prefer to use the word 'ethnicity' instead, yet this too is not without its problems. My family and I will all, correctly, tick the 'Asian: Other' box on any form enquiring about our ethnicity. And yet the extent to which we identify with that ethnic group (with its language, traditions and culture) is vastly different.

The language surrounding race is complex. It is related to identity and self-identity, the complex interplay between cultures and context—a complexity reflected in the fact that there is no clear consensus, even among those who are racially othered, about what is acceptable. Notwithstanding these complexities, I will continue to use the phrase *'racial diversity'*—as it is understood in our contemporary culture— as the categorization of people groups based on shared ethnic and cultural heritage.

The Day of Pentecost

Pentecost is the story of the birth of the church, a new people whose nature is unity in diversity. This event provides a blueprint for the church, displaying the essence of the content and character of Christ's body on earth. Jesus' disciples are filled with the Holy Spirit 'and began to speak in other tongues as the Spirit enabled them,' proclaiming the wonders of God (Acts 2.4). A multi-ethnic crowd is gathered in Jerusalem, who are amazed and perplexed to 'hear them declaring the wonders of God in our own tongues' (Acts 2.12). The church, despite all its shortcomings, is the realization of the kingdom of God on earth and this account provides inspiration for all those who want to take seriously the phrase in the Lord's Prayer that says, 'Thy kingdom come, thy will be done on earth as it is in heaven.' This truly inclusive vision for community applies to any institution where we want to see God's kingdom values at work and therefore must apply to our schools too.

Traditionally, theological reflection on these verses has focused on the miraculous nature of speaking in tongues and its impact on church history and tradition. This is not the whole story. Our understanding of this narrative has been shaped by a Western theological tradition, which has not always been able to see things from the perspective of one who speaks a different language from the dominant culture.

So, I would like to explore this passage from the viewpoint of someone who is not from the majority culture—from the aspect of an outsider, someone who sees in this passage a real affirmation of diversity and inclusion. I am indebted to the black theological tradition, and especially the work of Jennings, for illuminating to me an alternative way of looking at this story. This provides us with a number of important ideas related to what it means to value and embrace racial diversity.

Unity in Diversity Has Always been God's Idea

The events of Pentecost demonstrate that a racially diverse humanity, united in the worship of the one God, was a fulfilment of prophecy. So when people from all over the known world hear the disciples speak in their own mother tongue and are bewildered, Peter explains that these events are in accordance with the Scriptures: they were witnessing the dawn of a new age, heralded by the death and resurrection of Jesus, the fulfilment of God's plan (Act 2.16, 17).

A Divinely Initiated Departure from the Status Quo

Diversity and difference are now to be at the heart of the community of believers who are united in worship. This idea of a united but diverse community was so radical in nature that it could only have been the product of a divine initiative.

The world of the disciples, like our own, was marked by deep divisions and tensions—ethnic, class, gender, enslaved and free. In such an environment, a united community was almost impossible to conceive without the completely revolutionary outpouring of the Spirit of God. The radically universal nature of Jesus' ministry is now to define the ministry of his disciples too. The same Spirit is calling us today to create boundary-defying inclusive communities wherever we are placed.

The Gift of Tongues: An Image of Service and Relationship

The miraculous gift of tongues— which is about speaking the language of the other and hearing the gospel message in one's mother tongue—helps us to understand the character necessary for a truly diverse but united community.

At that first Pentecost, the coming of the Holy Spirit enables the gospel to be brought to those who hear it in their own language. Moving from east to west and north to south, and covering the key communities of the Jewish diaspora, Luke (the writer of Acts) presents the reader with an international crowd composed of visitors and residents in Jerusalem who are amazed to hear the gospel in their own tongue (Acts 2.6).

The language we speak is such a vital part of our identity: it is the way in which we make sense and express the world around us. Jennings compellingly argues that the Spirit creates deep connection through the intimate medium of language: 'The followers of Jesus are now being connected in a way that joins them to people in the most intimate space—of voice, memory, sound… to speak a language is to speak a people.'[11]

The act of speaking someone else's language is an expression of intimacy and relationality; it shows humility and submission; a willingness to enter the world of the other and learn from them.

> To learn a language requires submission to a people. Even if in the person of a single teacher, the learner must submit to that single voice, learning what the words mean as they are bound to events, songs, jokes, everyday practices, habits of mind and body, all within a land and the journey of a people.[12]

Similarly, we should approach those who are different with the same attitude that we would need if we were to speak their language—motivated by a humble desire to learn from the other, whilst checking our conscious or subconscious assumptions of our own perspective being superior.

The act of hearing someone else speaking your mother tongue, that most familiar language, is also significant. Our native language is our language of intimacy. When the gospel message was preached that first Pentecost, God chose the 'heart' language of each people group assembled there and, in doing so, affirmed the beauty of each culture present. This was a supreme example of unity in diversity; of genuinely including people by affirming what they hold most dear (in this case, their mother tongue), of giving each people group gathered there dignity and respect.

So How Does This Apply to Our Schools?

This vision of a radically inclusive, boundary-defying community should define our educational system. We should strive to enable every student and staff member staff to be a valued and equal member of the school community. Yet our schools operate within a normative white society with a legacy of colonialism which has left its mark—from the curriculum and resources to systems, structures and lines of power.

Pentecost reveals some of the crucial attitudes that are necessary to redress the balance: the celebration of diversity in creation; the need for humility in dealing with difference; the need to learn from others who are dissimilar to us; and the desire to affirm what is beautiful and precious in the other. In a world in which humans try to colonize and dominate, subjugating people and their cultures and suppressing all that is different, the Spirit of God shows a new way to live together.

Questions for Reflection

- How does the realization that every child is made in God's image impact the decisions that are made in the school and the interactions that happen?
- What might it look like to approach people (staff and students) who are different with an attitude of humility? How can the whole school community be engaged in learning from each other?
- How can you affirm and celebrate the God-given difference of the diverse cultures that are represented in your school or community?

3 Embracing Racial Diversity

Miroslav Volf's metaphor of 'embrace' offers a compelling vision for true racial diversity in schools that moves beyond the tokenistic. In his book *Exclusion and Embrace,* Volf provides 'a theological exploration of identity, otherness and reconciliation.'[13] Volf argues that 'identity and otherness' lie at the heart of any theological reflection on social interaction. It is this recognition that makes Volf's work so applicable regarding racial diversity in our schools, which is ultimately an issue of identity and otherness; it arises out of a desire to protect identity which often results in the exclusion of those perceived to be other.

This is a metaphor of reconciliation which requires all parties involved to put aside the prejudice that underlines racism (and all other forms of discrimination) and meet those who are different from us by relating to our common humanity:

> The will to give ourselves to others and 'welcome' them, to readjust our identities to make space for them, is prior to any judgment about others, except that of identifying them in their humanity.[14]

The foundation of this metaphor is deeply Christian and rooted in the nature of God: the mutual self-giving love that characterizes the relationship between the three persons of the Trinity, the 'outstretched arms of Christ on the cross' and 'the outstretched arms of the "father" receiving the "prodigal."'[15] This is a vision inspired by God's 'project with the world unveiled in Jesus Christ' and therefore applicable not just to Christians or the church but each and every situation where humans interact with each other.[16]

The Drama of Embrace

Volf's metaphor of embrace is a drama made of four acts, which form an integrated movement: 'opening the arms, waiting, closing the arms and opening them again.'[17] Each movement is required, and they must follow each other in order, for the embrace to happen.

Act One: Opening the Arms

The drama of embrace begins with open arms:

> Open arms are a gesture of the body reaching for the other. They are a sign of my discontent with my own self-enclosed identity, a code of desire for the other. I do not want to be a part of myself only; I want the other to be a part of who I am, and I want to be part of the other.[18]

The open arms relate to invitation and welcome but also a desire to learn from the other. How welcoming is the British educational system to those from diverse racial backgrounds? This is a question that is relevant not just to students but also members of staff.

Often, schools reflect the local demographic. However, the extent to which children and families of diverse racial backgrounds are made welcome in school, for who they are and what they bring to the table, varies from school to school and area to area. This question is particularly pertinent to schools with a predominantly monocultural community. The welcome and invitation may be sincere but there is neither the need, nor the awareness of the need, to learn from the other. Instead, it is often the case that the other assimilates into the dominant norm.

Perhaps a more revealing answer would be the extent to which this relates to teachers and governors and especially those in positions of senior leadership within the school. Is there a desire within the educational system to hear—and be influenced by—a diversity of voices? Is there a desire at every level of the system to learn from the other and, where necessary, the courage to change?

The numbers surrounding this question show there is still a long way to go: one in three students in England is from a non-white heritage and yet approximately only 8% of all teachers and just over 1% of all head teachers are from non-white ethnic backgrounds.[19] Paul Miller argues that 'A body of research has confirmed that race discrimination/race inequality is a factor in the progression of teachers of black, Asian and minority ethnic heritage in England.'[20] Jeffrey Boakye, in his book *I Heard What You Said,* provides an honest insight into his experience of being a black teacher in a white system, calling for an extensive audit of the entire educational climate, resulting in the removal of 'the jagged corners of institutional bias that threaten to injure black students and teachers every day.'[21] Until this happens, the welcome of the open arms has the potential to damage those it invites.

Act Two: Waiting

This next stage, of waiting, is important in acknowledging that this is a reciprocal relationship, in which both parties need to choose to participate. Volf explains what is involved in waiting:

> The open arms reach out but stop before touching the other. They wait... Before it can proceed, it must wait for the desire to arise in the other and for the arms to open.[22]

Having repeatedly expressed its desire to engage in racial diversity more intentionally, the education system is, in many ways, in this stage of waiting. It is waiting for those who have historically been damaged by the system to engage voluntarily in it. This is, ironically, a vulnerable position of powerlessness, which accepts that those from minority ethnic backgrounds may not want to be embraced, because of painful memories.

There are many who do not have the choice—countless parents and students are forced to engage with their local educational system due to lack of a viable alternative. My own experience as a parent resonates with this—there were so many times when I longed to disengage from an educational system that caused my children so much pain.

Waiting, however, is not passive; both parties have work to do. Moving from waiting to embrace requires the perpetrator of injustice to reflect on history and practice, and often requires repentance. As Volf explains, 'The embrace itself—full reconciliation—cannot take place until the truth has been said and justice done.'[23] Volf argues that both victims and perpetrators need to seek forgiveness: the idea of the non innocence of the victim is contentious within a context of the continued racial marginalization of minorities. However, to move forward, anger and unforgiveness need to be put aside so that they no longer define relationships. Hard work needs to be done, in relation to structural racism and the breakdown of trust between those racial minorities and the educational system, if waiting is to lead to embrace.

Act Three: Closing the Arms

Closing the arms, the goal of the embrace, is a reciprocal action that is both active (holding) and passive (being held):

> In the embrace a host is a guest and a guest is a host. Though one may receive or give more than the other, each must enter the space of the other, feel the presence of the other, and make its own presence felt.[24]

Where no space has been created for the other, true reciprocity is not possible.

In relation to racial diversity, the movement has been predominantly one way—the acceptance of the other into the educational system, whilst not creating enough opportunities for that presence to be felt in a meaningful way. Work needs to be done to make the presence of racial minorities felt in every aspect of school life—from leadership and the representation of staff and governors, to decolonizing the curriculum, to creating space in which minority ethnic pupils and staff can be authentic and contribute without fear of a fragile white response. Moreover, there is the need to interrogate the systemic racism that prevents this presence from being felt; there is the need to be intentionally anti-racist.

Volf anticipates the danger of a one-sided embrace, arguing for the necessity of a soft touch:

> I may not close my arms around the other too tightly, so as to crush her and assimilate her...Similarly, I must keep the boundaries of my own self firm, offer resistance, otherwise I will be engaged in a self-destructive act of abnegation.[25]

This is an important reminder that embracing racial diversity will always involve the tension between holding onto cultural heritage, while making space and allowing the identity of the other to shape the shared space. There also needs to be a clear understanding that embrace is about equality and sharing in a common space and that, whilst the default is white, this embrace may remain one sided. As Boakye argues, whiteness needs to be decentred, with the understanding that:

> Dominant whiteness actually victimizes everyone. This includes white people who are blinded by the glare and numbed to its sting, failing to see the racism that their whiteness ideologically relies on.[26]

Act Four: Opening the Arms Again

The final act of embrace, opening the arms again, is important to preserve authenticity:

> The opening of the arms underlies that, although the other may be inscribed into the self, the alterity may not be neutralized into an undifferentiated 'we.'[27]

The metaphor of the open arms reminds us that we are not trying to create a homogenous space within our schools where everyone must share the same identity, values, ideas and cultures. Rather, we are aiming to allow people to be authentic and not feel that they need to assimilate to belong. These open arms remind us that the drama of embrace will happen repeatedly as we engage with the other and learn from them, creating a more diverse space in which difference is celebrated.

Questions for Reflection

- How welcoming does your school appear to someone who is not from the majority culture? Do they see themselves represented in any way in the school environment: in the displays, the curriculum or in the teaching staff?
- Boakye argues that 'dominant whiteness actually victimizes everyone.' To what extent do you agree?
- How can we be intentional in creating a culture of embrace where each student feels able to be themselves?

National Perspectives for Local Change

4

'We take racism seriously…'

My husband and I were sitting across the table, speaking to a member of middle management in our son's school. We were discussing a particularly troubling comment made by a teacher, his concern that my 14-year-old son would take part in terrorist activities. Inexperienced as we were at dealing with the educational system on issues of race and not wanting to make a fuss, when we first heard about this incident, we told our son to report it at school. The issue was resolved quickly the very next day: when asked on the phone whether he had made the comment, the teacher in question denied it. My son was told that that was the end of the matter and no further action would be taken.

So, the comment by the member of middle management about taking racism seriously would have been a welcome one, had it not been for the fact that the person who initially resolved the issue was none other than the person sitting in front of us. She immediately offered to investigate it further…

This incident displays the complex set of issues at stake in conversations on race in schools:

- an educational system, underpinned by a legal, statutory framework and philosophy, which promotes equality and inclusion;
- a school system that wants to be seen to be doing the right thing;
- individual members of staff who consciously or unconsciously have their own biases; and
- parents of ethnic minority children who have to navigate the white normative system successfully, balancing the need for justice and equal opportunity with the need for diplomacy and the desire not to create more trouble for their own children.

There is a tension between doing the right thing and being seen to do the right thing. I believe that schools *do* want to create a more inclusive and diverse environment where everyone thrives. Yet, faced with the challenge of navigating the complex landscape of racism and diversity, many are content with being *seen* to do the right thing; ticking the boxes but failing to deal with racial injustice and the real lack of diversity that exists.

The Statutory Framework

Statutory and legal frameworks have been provided in law, whilst the impact of a Christian vision for implementing inclusivity and diversity is evaluated by the SIAMS (Statutory Inspection of Anglican and Methodist Schools) framework. These will be explored briefly before considering how they are applied in practice.

The statutory framework for education provides a clear foundation for building a culture of racial diversity. The Equality Act of 2010 legally protects people from discrimination based on nine 'protected characteristics.'[28] Equality and diversity are considered critical to the Department of Education's vision:

> We enable children...to thrive by protecting the vulnerable and ensuring the delivery of excellent standards of education, training and care. This helps realize everyone's potential—and that powers our economy, strengthens society and increases fairness.[29]

The extent to which this vision is realized is assessed by Ofsted, which makes a holistic judgment. Its latest equality objectives explain that 'Ofsted will give due regard to equality, diversity and inclusion during inspection and regulation and in its research and evaluation work.'[30] In making these judgments in schools, assessment will be in relation to both compliance 'with their relevant duties under the Equality Act 2010' and promotion, that is, 'the extent to which they promote British values and promote equality and diversity.'[31]

The 'British values' mentioned above are considered the basic values that undergird British society and aim to prepare children to become responsible members of modern Britain: 'Democracy, the rule of law, individual liberty and mutual respect and tolerance for those of different faiths and beliefs.'[32] This central emphasis on providing an education suitable for *all* students, preparing them to become responsible members of modern-day Britain, underpins an educational vision that embraces diversity.

The Church of England 'Vision for Education'

As the established church, the Church of England occupies a unique position within this country, with its vision to be 'a Christian presence in every community.' As such, its *Vision for Education* is all-encompassing: 'Deeply Christian, Serving the Common Good.' As the foreword explains, this 'is not just a vision for Church of England schools, but a Church of England vision for education.' This Christian vision is centred around Jesus' promise of 'life in all its fullness' and is holistic in its remit, embracing the 'spiritual, physical, intellectual, emotional, moral and social development of children and young people.'[33]

It is a vision of human flourishing that generously embraces difference at its core and one that is deeply pertinent to the educational establishment:

> It is hospitable to diversity, respects freedom of religion and belief, and encourages others to contribute from the depths of their own traditions and understanding. It invites collaboration, alliances, negotiation of differences and the forming of new settlements in order to serve the flourishing of a healthy plural society and democracy, together with a healthily plural educational system.[34]

This vision is permeated by four elements: educating for wisdom, hope, community and dignity. In particular, the third and fourth elements provide a vision for education that promotes a culture of diversity, in which each individual is valued, whilst the fostering of good relationships is central to communal life. There is so much in this vision that resonates with Volf's metaphor of embrace, a few key elements of which will be considered below.

The Anglican vision not only recognizes the intrinsic worth of every student, but also the uniqueness of identity:

> Each is to be understood as respectfully and deeply as possible; to be encouraged to stretch themselves spiritually, morally, intellectually, imaginatively and actively, and to aspire to be well-educated.[35]

This is not a one-size-fits-all model of education but allows each student to be authentic and preserve their identity. Following Jesus' example and teaching, this vision for education pays close attention to the marginalized, vulnerable and excluded and considers how schools can ensure that all are valued.

There is also an acknowledgment of the way in which our lived experience and our interactions with others changes and shapes our own identity, with an inherent tension between holding on to one's identity and being open to being changed:

> The wisdom tradition offers models for staying true to our roots while being hospitably open. This uniting of the given and the found—what has been given by the past and what is found in the present through experience, new events, new knowledge and other people—is a challenge to every tradition, every society and every education system.

This provides space for the healthy debate, agreement and disagreement that are part of embracing difference.

The vision has a communal as well as individual dimension: 'The conviction that we are created and sustained by God for living together in families and communities is at the root of our dedication to educating for life together.[36] There is a realistic acceptance about 'how much can and does go wrong' and the need for reconciliation, as 'a crucial element of wisely negotiating the multi-layered and diverse reality of the society in which we live.'[37] In particular, it is recognized that dealing with difference lies at the heart of living well together:

> It is not too difficult to honour the dignity of those who seem to be 'one of us,' similar to ourselves, 'normal' by our own measure. The challenge is how we treat those who seem alien, abnormal, disturbingly or dangerously different. How schools deal with such difference is a crucial indicator of quality.[38]

Inspired Leaders

The central importance of developing inspirational leaders to realize this vision is articulated in *Called, Connected, Committed: 24 Leadership Practices for Educational Leaders,* which identifies the inherent benefits of embracing diversity:[39]

> An authentic Christian vision for living well together is one that is scandalously inclusive: where all are welcomed, and where everyone gets to play a part...Diverse teams do not simply tick boxes or fulfil targets. We think, lead, teach and learn better because of our diversity.[40]

At the same time, it is recognized that this requires an honest acceptance of what has happened historically and the need for intentionality in moving forward:

> While leaders embrace opportunities to celebrate living and learning together, they recognize that the chequered history of faith-based inclusion usually requires particular attention to ethos, pedagogy, curriculum, appointments and use of resources in order to counter stereotypes of judgment, unjust discrimination, and often unconscious bias in relation to gender, sexuality, ethnicity, class and relations among faith groups. The dignity and integrity of each must be respected and good practices can form generations to come, helping to redefine community, replace division, foster reconciliation and shape ways of living better together.[41]

From Lament to Action

The publication of the Church of England's 'From Lament to Action' report (April 2021) highlighted that there was still much work to be done. A year after the death of George Floyd, this report reflected on racial justice across the church and made several recommendations required to achieve lasting change. Central to this report was the recognition that the church was still deeply institutionally racist and the fact that decades of recommendations, reports, discussions and debates had failed to bring about sufficient progress in the area of racial justice.[42]

Education was highlighted as one of the areas where change was needed. The report recognized the church as 'one of the nation's significant education providers' and that, 'despite various affirmative steps and developing a comprehensive vision for education, various groups have repeatedly pointed out its lack of robust initiatives to highlight racial diversity and anti-racism work.' Here, as in other areas of church, there was a need to implement 'significant cultural and structural change.'[43] With this in mind, we turn now to think about what practical things can be done in our schools in order to create an environment that truly embraces racial diversity.

Questions for Reflection

- What difference should a Christian vision for education make to our pursuit of racial justice?
- To what extent do you think that the promotion of British values supports the embrace of diversity? To what extent can it impede progress?
- Do you agree that 'we think, lead, teach and learn better because of our diversity'?

5 Beyond Tokenism: Towards Embracing Racial Diversity

> We should all know that diversity makes for a rich tapestry, and we must understand that all the threads of the tapestry are equal in value no matter what their colour.
>
> Maya Angelou

True diversity is about a culture that intrinsically values difference. So, if we are to move beyond the tokenistic, it is essential that we pause and reflect on our motivation for promoting diversity. Is it because we believe that it is the correct thing to do, or do we 'pursue it and chase it down because it is inherently better'?[44] If we are not inspired by the beauty, strength and other benefits that result from an embrace of diversity, these actions will fail to impact the culture of an organization significantly.

Our education system intends to educate our young people to be responsible citizens of modern multicultural Britain and so it is vital that *all* schools prioritize the embrace of diversity. This is particularly important in predominantly monocultural schools, where the lack of diversity in the staff and student body is seen as a reason not to do so, with the attendant attitude that 'this is not really an issue for us.' Embracing diversity is an even more pressing issue in these contexts; it is not only necessary to prepare white students for life in more diverse contexts, but also to help those racially isolated minority ethnic students feel represented in the life of the school.

Changing culture takes time. It also involves intentionality and a multi-faceted approach, which normalizes the change that at first seems novel or even radical. This kind of effort is not a top-down approach but requires all stakeholders to collaborate in moving forward. Moreover, as the metaphor of embrace reminds us, this is about a change in attitude; it is about embracing otherness / difference in a humble posture of mutuality, being prepared to give *and* receive and to be changed through the process.

Outlined below are some of the key actions that are necessary to build a culture that embraces diversity.

Evaluate the Culture

> If you want to know what water is like, don't ask the fish.
>
> Chinese proverb

Context is everything and the first step is to evaluate the culture of a school in relation to diversity. This is easier said than done, especially for those who are used to operating within one cultural framework, where white is normal and everyone else fits in. In this framework white privilege operates as an invisible force. If you are white, you are possibly not even aware of it. If you are non-white, you are aware of it in the many small and large decisions you make on a daily basis, from the availability of products that match your skin tone to the unconscious judgments people make based on the colour of your skin.

An honest acceptance and acknowledgment of the extent to which a school is normatively white should be a starting point towards building a culture that embraces diversity.

Listen Well and Speak Courageously

Listening well is about providing a space in which everyone can respectfully express difference, knowing that they are safe to do so and that they are heard. However, as DiAngelo reminds us through the concept of white fragility, any conversation about race is prone to a fragile and often negative or defensive response. This needs to be acknowledged and everyone needs to listen without defensiveness, be willing to admit where they have been wrong and how they can learn from the other.

Space needs to be created and modelled well by those in authority. Space is established by developing a culture that listens well to all involved in the conversation. In the hierarchical context of a school, it is especially important to listen well to those who lack authority: listening to all students but particularly those who are marginalized or vulnerable due to their otherness. Listening well is an active choice that invariably involves some follow-up action.

Schools also need to be safe places to explore and learn, allowing people to challenge and question respectfully without the fear of being labelled as prejudiced or racist. Too many genuine conversations on contentious and sensitive issues fail to take place for fear of saying the wrong thing. Young people need space to explore difficult issues respectfully—this is part of education's role. Leaders need to engage with difficult issues, not avoid them—this is learning to be comfortable with the uncomfortable.

Challenging the *status quo* is never easy and can be costly. However, if injustice is to be challenged, if equity is to be embraced, it needs us all to speak courageously. This requires perseverance, because all too often the response is not outright hostility but polite indifference—the kind of 'Thank you for your contribution' comment that goes no further than the meeting room. So, there is a need to persist. Too often, I find myself in a group of white people, saying the same thing repeatedly and seeing little impact, yet the need to speak out remains as strong as ever.

Make Representation Count

The presence of non-white leaders and teachers is a prophetic presence, signalling a willingness of the system to lay down power and espouse its dearly held ideals of equality and diversity. Systemic change can only occur when diverse people have distinctive and authoritative voices within the system. This is about normalizing the presence of diversity in predominantly white spaces; authoritative, diverse voices and variety of thought are essential for this to happen.

This change, however, will not happen naturally, requiring initiatives such as the Church of England's *Leaders Like Us* programme for aspiring head teachers, to overcome the barriers that have historically prevented this from occurring. Similarly, every school needs a proactive strategy to recruit, enable and encourage authoritative, diverse voices to be heard and to impact the life of the school.

The adage that 'You can't be what you can't see' is particularly true in education and this co-identification helps draw minority ethnic students into the teaching profession.[45] However, such representation is not just about the future, it is also about the present—it is having people within the teaching and governing body who understand what it means to be racially other and who can draw on their own experience to challenge discrimination and create a more inclusive space.

Initial efforts at working towards diversity may appear tokenistic and it often unfairly puts the burden of diversity onto a few individuals. However, at times, this pain barrier of tokenism is necessary in order to begin the move forward, especially if those actions can be reframed as positive affirmations of diversity. After all, 'A journey of a thousand miles begins with a single step' (Chinese philosopher, Lao Tzu).

Is the Curriculum Fit for Purpose?

The curriculum is a key area in which diversity can be embraced within the life of the school. Developing an inclusive and decolonized course of study focuses on the need to contextualize the curriculum to meet *all* students' needs. Historically, 'white' has been the default norm when constructing and implementing the curriculum. An inclusive curriculum decentres this focus, rebalancing that power to represent a diversity of voices and perspectives. This is not about erasing history but retelling it in a way that acknowledges, critically examines and redresses the influence of the colonial legacy on what and how we teach. Similarly, diversifying the curriculum is about telling the human story from a variety of different perspectives, not just a Western eurocentric one. As Boakye explains:

> Non-white perspectives are vital if the taught curriculum is to have any true integrity. Otherwise, it will forever fall victim to itself, blind to its own shortcomings and flaws and limited to a cultural and ideological vocabulary of its own invention.[46]

A diversity audit, identifying examples of diversity in the curriculum, teaching resources and the learning environment, is an effective first step. Moving forwards, there is a clear need for intentionality in filling the gaps, which will invariably involve thinking outside the box and ensuring that diverse topics, voices and resources are used and become commonplace in our schools.

Racial Justice: Underachievement, Exclusions

Frequently, statistics relating to school exclusion rates and underachievement point to a racial bias at the heart of the education system. Acknowledging the racial inequalities that persist, Bhopal explains that:

> School experiences are crucial in the transition to further and higher education and access to the labour market, yet black and minority ethnic groups continue to remain disadvantaged in these transitions.[47]

These inequalities need to be countered through relevant training, including unconscious bias training and strategies that promote anti-racism. And this, as Boakye argues, is the responsibility of everyone, and especially every teacher:

> If we are ever going to achieve an equitable education system, it demands that teachers of all backgrounds are active in their challenging of the *status quo* and sensitive to inequality, prejudice and bias at every level.[48]

Questions for Reflection

- How can you intentionally create opportunities for your school community to listen well and speak courageously?
- How can you make representation count in your context?
- What steps can you take to diversify the curriculum?

6 Concluding Reflections

> After this I looked, and there before me was a great multitude that no one could count, from every nation, tribe, people and language standing before the throne and before the Lamb.
>
> Rev 7.9

A Christian vision for embracing racial diversity should be rooted in God's vision for the interaction between diverse humanity, as envisaged in that glorious image of the rainbow people of God we see in Revelation. It is an inspirational picture of inclusivity and diversity that will characterize the new heaven and new earth. The crowd is diverse in nature, drawn from 'every nation, tribe, people and language,' but united in the worship of Jesus, the Lamb of God. This is a vision of what will be but also about what could be as we strive to make God's kingdom a reality 'on earth as it is in heaven.'

Volf reminds us that God's vision for this interaction between diverse humans involves holding in tension what is precious about one's own identity, whilst being open to learn, grow and be changed for the better through our interactions with others who are different:

> God's project with the world unveiled in Jesus Christ...is to make the world into God's home and thereby also into the home of God's creatures—each creature unique and locally rooted and each... constitutively open to all others, both indwelling in them and being indwelled by them.[49]

This dynamic interaction is part of the way in which all, made in God's image, get a fuller sense of who we are meant to be. It is essential if we are to see beyond our own cultures and identities to other expressions of what it means to be a human being, reflecting God's image, and to be transformed by that encounter.

It is this recognition of the fluidity of identity and mutual self-giving that makes Volf's metaphor so relevant to the conversation on a Christian vision for embracing diversity in schools today. The active process of embrace moves us beyond tokenism, deepening encounter and leading to transformation.

Our educational system needs to recognize its own fluidity and be willing to embrace an identity which is no longer primarily tied to whiteness. This will require intentionality in making space for the other and the forfeiting of power and privilege. It is only then that the pursuit of racial diversity will move beyond the tokenistic to become an embrace that is transformative and life-enhancing, enabling us all to flourish and fulfil our God-given potential.

Notes

1 L E Swaner and A Wolfe, *Flourishing Together: A Christian Vision for Students, Educators and Schools* (Grand Rapids, MI: Eerdmans, 2021) p 4.

2 Cited in K Bhopal and Y Alibhai-Brown, *White Privilege: The Myth of a Post-Racial Society* (Bristol: Policy Press, 2018) p 65.

3 The work of Prof Paul Miller highlights the continued systemic inequality within our educational system: P Miller, '"System Conditions," System Failure, Structural Racism and Anti-Racism in the United Kingdom: Evidence from Education and Beyond,' *Societies* 11, no 2 (7 May 2021): 42, doi:10.3390/soc11020042

4 D Mckesson: 'Equity vs Equality in Tech. Which Is Fair?' Black Enterprise (30 October 2017) https://www.blackenterprise.com/video-deray-mckesson-equity-vs-equality-tech/

5 N Shukla (ed), *The Good Immigrant* (London: Unbound, 2016) argues that 'the biggest burden facing people of colour in this country is that society deems us bad immigrants...until we cross over in their consciousness, through popular culture, winning races, baking good cakes, being conscientious doctors, to become good immigrants.'

6 L Saad and R DiAngelo explore this concept further in *Me and White Supremacy* (London: Quercus Publishing, 2022).

7 R DiAngelo, *White Fragility* (London: Penguin, 2019).

8 https://www.bbc.co.uk/bitesize/guides/zdrxbdm/revision/4

9 W J Jennings, *The Christian Imagination* (New Haven, CT: Yale University Press, 2010); J K Carter, *Race: A Theological Account* (Oxford University Press, 2008).

10 For example, Carter's work illustrates how 'the discourse of theology aided and abetted the processes by which "man" came to be viewed as a modern racial being.' *ibid*, p 3.

11 W J Jennings, 'Acts,' *Belief: A Theological Commentary on the Bible* (Louisville, KY: Westminster John Knox Press, 2017) p 28.

12 *ibid*, p 29.

13 M Volf, *Exclusion and Embrace: A Theological Exploration of Identity, Otherness, and Reconciliation*, Revised and updated (Nashville, TN: Abingdon Press, 2019).

14 *ibid*, p xxiii.

15 *ibid*, p 19.

16 *ibid*, p xxiii.

17 *ibid*, p 143.

18 *ibid*.

19 P W Miller, 'Tackling Race Inequality in School Leadership: Positive Actions in BAME Teacher Progression— Evidence from Three English Schools,' *Educational*

Management Administration and Leadership 48, no 6 (November 2020): 986–1006, doi:10.1177/1741143219873098

20 *ibid.*

21 J Boakye, *I Heard What You Said* (London: Picador, 2022) p 352.

22 M Volf, *Exclusion and Embrace, op cit,* p 144, p 145.

23 *ibid*, p 20.

24 *ibid*, p 146.

25 *ibid*, p 146.

26 J Boakye, *I Heard What You Said, op cit,* p 352.

27 M Volf, *Exclusion and Embrace, op cit,* p 146.

28 The nine protected characteristics in the UK are age, disability, gender reassignment, marriage and civil partnership, pregnancy and maternity, race, religion or belief, sex and sexual orientation.

29 'Equality and Diversity: Department of Education,' https://www.gov.uk/government/organisations/department-for-education/about/equality-and-diversity

30 'Ofsted's Equality Objectives 2020 to 2022,' https://www.gov.uk/government/publications/ofsteds-equality-objectives-2020-to-2022/ofsteds-equality-objectives-2020-to-2022

31 *ibid.*

32 Tolerance itself is about respecting the views of others and not imposing our own; however, tolerance is only the first step in the embrace of difference which is also about engaging positively with that difference and celebrating it.

33 'Church of England Vision for Education,' p 2, https://cofefoundation.contentfiles.net/media/assets/file/Church_of_England_Vision_for_Education_-_2016_jdYA7EO.pdf

34 *ibid*, p 9.

35 *ibid*, p 10.

36 *ibid*, p 11.

37 *ibid*, p 10.

38 *ibid*, p 12.

39 D F Ford and A Wolfe, 'Called, Connected, Committed,' https://cofefoundation.contentfiles.net/media/assets/file/Called_Connected_Committed_-_David_Ford_and_Andy_Wolfe.pdf

40 *ibid*, p 32.

41 *ibid.*

42 'From Lament to Action,' 11, https://www.churchofengland.org/sites/default/files/2021-04/FromLamentToAction-report.pdf

43 *ibid*, p 4.

44 D F Ford and A Wolfe, 'Called, Connected, Committed,' *op cit,* p 32.

45 P Miller, '"White Sanction," Institutional, Group and Individual Interaction in the Promotion and Progression of Black and Minority Ethnic Academics and Teachers in England,' *Power and Education* 8, no 3 (November 2016): 205–21, doi:10.1177/1757743816672880

46 J Boakye, *I Heard What You Said, op cit,* p 182.

47 K Bhopal and Y Alibhai-Brown, *White Privilege, op cit*, p 65.

48 J Boakye, *I Heard What You Said, op cit,* p 351.

49 M Volf, *Exclusion and Embrace, op cit,* p xxiii.